Women's Voices from Kurdistan

A Selection of Kurdish Poetry

This beautiful and groundbreaking collection of English translations from Gorani, Sorani, Kurmanji, and Arabic was achieved through an innovative collaborative translation project in the Centre for Kurdish Studies, University of Exeter. From the nineteenth to the twenty-first century, it expresses women's voices on politics, nationalism, gender, love, science, education, and everyday Kurdishness in memory, elegy, dream, and discourse. See such haunting lines from Gulîzer as "May those who have stayed not say the leaving is easy./ May those who have left not say the staying is simple." Or "When two rivers separate/ How do they part their water?" Anyone interested in women's poetry, diaspora, translation, and transnation will want to hear these poems.

- Professor Regenia Gagnier FBA, author of *Literatures of Liberalization: Global Circulation and the Long Nineteenth Century* and editor of *The Global Circulation Project;* Department of English and Film, University of Exeter, UK.

The vivid image of love, lost, hope, beauty, desire, violence, pain, and suffering that are sketched in this book enchant and attract readers to enter into a more intimate lives of Kurdish women. In this exquisite collection of poems written by Kurdish women and translated into English for the first time, we are exposed to a more imaginative way of hearing Kurdish women's voices. It is in the interstices of lived words and the lifeworld that Kurdish women poets candidly dream freedom and suggest ways to move beyond all forms of oppression and violence.

- Professor Shahrzad Mojab, University of Toronto, Canada and the editor of *Women of Non-State Nation: The Kurds.*

Women's Voices from Kurdistan

A Selection of Kurdish Poetry

Editors:

Farangis Ghaderi

Clémence Scalbert Yücel

Yaser Hassan Ali

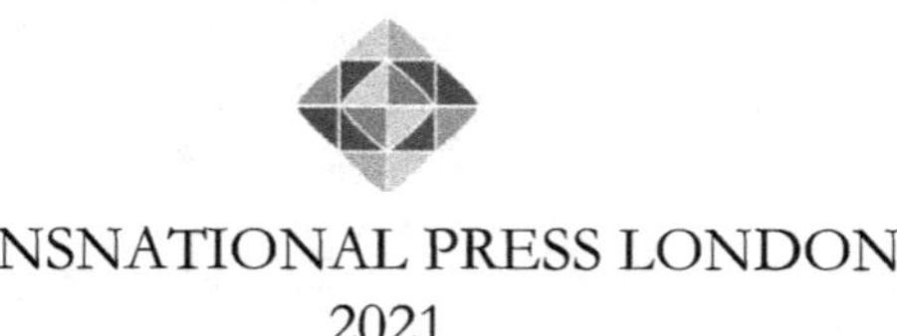

TRANSNATIONAL PRESS LONDON
2021

Heritage Series: 4

Women's Voices from Kurdistan - A Selection of Kurdish Poetry

Editors: Farangis Ghaderi, Clémence Scalbert Yücel, Yaser Hassan Ali

Translation Editor: Rinat Harel

First Published in 2021 by TRANSNATIONAL PRESS LONDON in the United Kingdom, 12 Ridgeway Gardens, London, N6 5XR, UK.
www.tplondon.com

Paperback
ISBN: 978-1-912997-81-7
Digital
ISBN: 978-1-80135-033-4

Cover Design: Nihal Yazgan
Cover Art: Rounak Rasoulpoor

www.tplondon.com

Contents

Acknowledgements

We are thankful to the British Institute for the Study of Iraq whose financial support, through an outreach grant, enabled us to realise this work. The Centre for Kurdish Studies at the University of Exeter also supported this project.

We thank all the participants in the workshop who worked along with us to create such a creative and inspiring momentum: Yunus Abakay, Jaber Al-Ahmari, Mohammed Asiri, Michelle Bolduc, Marouf Cabi, Kawa Ghobadi, Alana Levinson-Labrosse, Eliana Maestri, Asmaa Meftah, Karwan Osman, Abla Oudeh, Christina Philips, Christine Robins. Our thanks also go to Lara Radusin and Daisy Vaughan who joined us following the workshop, to Kawa Morad who answered a few queries concerning Kurmanji poems, to Jaffer Sheyholislami for his comments on the translation of 'Memory of Shirin' and to Bahar Hosseini for sharing Jîla Huseynî's photo and biography. Among others, our special gratitude to Michelle Bolduc for supporting, advising, and working with us throughout the project, giving us confidence and strength.

Translating Kurdish Poetry as a Collective Endeavour

Farangis Ghaderi and Clémence Scalbert Yücel

Kurdish literature has remained little known and little studied outside Kurdistan until very recently. Few pioneer studies were dedicated to oral literature, but Kurdish written classical and contemporary literature did not attract the interest of Western scholars for a long time. In the past decade however, the study of Kurdish literature has developed and strengthened in a few universities outside Kurdistan.[1]

As scholars of literature, we read, study, and write about Kurdish literature and Kurdish authors and poets. Yet their works are rarely translated and remain mostly unknown to the wider readership. This situation could be explained by the fact that Kurdish is a minority language that has been little known and little studied and also suppressed and banned in the countries where Kurds live. With Kurdish being a minority language, and (up until recently in Iraq) not an official state language, there has been little support for translating Kurdish literature in Kurdistan or elsewhere in the world. Many literary translations that are produced as part of doctoral researches remain inaccessible to a wide audience since they often stay unpublished. Even when the outcome of such researches is published as academic articles, only extracts of translated texts are published and they are circulated mostly among the academic audiences. Furthermore, because the purpose of such translations is to develop an analysis

[1] For instance, nine PhD dissertations on Kurdish literature have been defended at the Centre for Kurdish Studies at the University of Exeter in the last decade. One can also mention the important role played by the Section for Kurdish Studies at the Jagiellonian University in Krakow.

and illustrate an argument, scholars often translate without reflecting on the actual practice of literary translation.

This lack of reflection also stems from the fact that many of the current students and scholars of Kurdish literature in British universities are non-native English speakers who are not very confident in producing what would be considered a 'good' translation. 'Anxieties about a "lack of fluency" in one or both languages' (noted by Corine Tachtiris in the case of immigrants in the USA)[2] prevents non-native English speakers from picturing themselves as literary translators. Additionally, their access to literary publishers in the UK or the USA is limited. Nonetheless, their work contributes to building an important body of Kurdish literature in the English language and offers samples of a variety of genres and styles to Anglophone readers. We gradually realised that by building on the strengths of such practices and the texts they have produced, we could make Kurdish literature accessible to a wider Anglophone audience, as well as build confidence and raise awareness on the practices of translation among researchers and students.

Against this backdrop, together with Alana Levinson-Labrosse (a published poet, and a translator, who was then a student of Kurdish Studies at the University of Exeter) we decided to organise a translation workshop in 2017 at the University of Exeter. Translation was part of our commitment to researching Kurdish literature and making it available to a broader audience.

The two-day workshop was funded by an outreach grant from the British Institute for the Study of Iraq and the Centre for Kurdish Studies and took place in Exeter in May 2018. Given the source of our funding, our selected literature originated mainly

---

[2] Tachtiris, C. (2019) 'Allyship and Intersectional Feminism in Translation'. The paper was presented at the Translating Women Conference, London, 31 October-1 November 2019, published as 'Translating women - activism in action', Institute of Translation and Interpretation, 3 August 2020, https://www.iti.org.uk/resource/translating-women---activism-in-action.html.

from Iraqi Kurdistan, and each of the participants brought to the table their own selection of texts which they chose according to their personal tastes, areas of expertise and interests, or research needs. Hence the diversity of our selected poems, which include nineteenth to twenty-first-century texts, and range from renowned nationalist poets to emerging writers from the Bahdinan region in Iraqi Kurdistan. However, we had decided that the chosen texts should engage with the general theme of women in Kurdish poetry. We also strived to select poems written by women poets so as to give voice to lesser-known writers.

We aimed to exhibit the diversity of Kurdish languages and dialects used by Kurdish poets throughout various time periods and geographical locations. This included Sorani Kurdish, Bahdinani Kurdish (a variant of Kurmanji spoken in Iraq), the endangered dialect of Kurdish Gorani, and also Arabic, a language used by some Kurdish poets in Iraq. As Kurdish is a repressed and banned minority language, Kurdish writers also use the dominant and official language of the states in which they live. Translating Arabic texts also enabled us to bring to this workshop students and scholars of Arabic literature who were unfamiliar with Kurdish literature. This was a great opportunity to develop interconnections, synergies, and interest across disciplines and language barriers that are unfortunately rarely crossed. Therefore, the poetry presented in this book does not claim to represent Kurdish poetry as a whole but aims to introduce a variety of rarely heard voices from different Kurdish dialects, historical periods, influences, and styles.

Based on preexisting models of translation workshops, we aimed to group together scholars of Kurdish literature with English native speakers who were not necessarily familiar with the original languages.[3] By doing so, we chose an established model in which the source language speakers first produce a

[3] In the groups working on texts in Arabic, everyone had access to and 'fluency' in both source and target languages.

'literal' translation that was to be 'refined' by target language speakers. We therefore used a collaborative model which had been used quite extensively and enabled the translation of literary texts in rare/minority languages in the absence of professional translators. We also invited translation studies scholars, Michelle Bolduc and Eliana Maestri, who introduced us to theoretical debates and practical issues related to literary and poetry translation.

Following the workshop, four of the participants, ourselves together with Yaser Hassan Ali (then a doctoral researcher in Kurdish literature) and Rinat Harel (a writer and a doctoral researcher in creative writing), continued to meet and work together on a regular basis, polishing some of the drafts produced during the workshop, and producing new translations. We presented some of our work to our local communities at the Exeter Respect Festival in May 2018 and May 2019, and the Exeter Literary Festival in November 2018.

With the publication of the outcome of the workshop, we hope to raise awareness of Kurdish poetry and its diverse voices within world literary circles. Moreover, we hope that our work will encourage Kurdish speakers to develop confidence engaging in translation practices and perhaps even to consider becoming professional literary translators.

Reflecting on our own practice, including the workshop and the preparation for this book, we have gained new insights and critical views on some established practices such as co-translation, which, while it can be useful in the short term, is not without pitfalls[4]. It can reproduce the situation of language domination and create a hierarchy between actors involved in the process; in blurring the roles, it often minimises, and even erases, the contribution of the native speaker.[5] The widespread emphasis

[4] See Ghaderi, F. and Scalbert Yücel, C. (2021). 'An Etat Présent of the Kurdish Literature in English Translation'. *The Translator*. DOI: 10.1080/13556509.2021.1872196

[5] On this issue, see for instance Calleja, J. and Collins, S. (2019). 'She Knows Too Much:

on fluency and readability that haunts literary translations knocks the confidence of the native Kurdish speaker. Therefore, the version they produce might be considered too 'literal' and would need to be polished and embellished by English native speakers and/or poets who are often credited as the translators. In this volume, we have been mindful of these issues when presenting the roles of translators, co-translators (when all parties have access to both source and target languages), and translation editor (with whom translators have had in-depth discussions on the best way of rendering the poems). Conscious of the various forms and practices of invisibilisation of the Kurdish language through time, it was important for us to give space to the original languages in this volume, hence the choice of a bilingual publication. While this work is the first step, we hope that it will inspire critical discussions, engagement, and maybe new forms and practices of translation for Kurdish literature.

"Bridge Translations," "Literal Translations," and Long-Term Harm'. *Asymptote* 2019 https://www.asymptotejournal.com/special-feature/jen-calleja-sophie-collins-she-knows-too-much

Unsung Poets of Kurdistan: A Reflection on Women's Voices in Kurdish Poetry

Farangis Ghaderi and Clémence Scalbert-Yücel

As a rich, ancient, and varied tradition, comprised of oral, classical, and modern forms,[1] Kurdish poetry is portrayed as a genre largely dominated by male poets. This stands in contradiction with the fact that female poets have played an important role in the development of Kurdish poetry, in particular modern poetry, a role that has remained mostly unacknowledged.[2] The marginalisation of women's voices is evident in the anthologies of Kurdish poetry,[3] historiographical accounts of Kurdish literature, and academic studies on Kurdish poetry,[4] and translations of Kurdish literature. Our recent study of English translations of Kurdish literature revealed that women are highly underrepresented and female poets constitute a marginal portion of the translated works.[5] While the significance

[1] On Kurdish poetry, see Ghaderi, F. (2016). *The Emergence and Development of Modern Kurdish Poetry*. PhD Dissertation. Exeter: University of Exeter.

[2] One of the few works on Kurdish women poets is Hassan, S. (2015). *Women and Literature: A Feminist Reading of Kurdish Women's Poetry*. PhD Dissertation. Exeter: University of Exeter.

[3] On poetry anthologies in Kurdish, see Ghaderi, F. (2015). 'The Challenges of Writing Kurdish Literary History'. *Kurdish Studies* 3(1): 3-25. On Anthologies in English translation see Ghaderi, F. and Scalbert Yücel, C. 'An Etat Présent of the Kurdish Literature in English Translation'. *The Translator* (2021), and our unpublished presentation at the Translating Women Conference, London, 31 October-1 November 2019, 'Bridging Activism and Scholarship: Translating Kurdish Women's Texts into English'.

[4] Most of the recent works on contemporary Kurdish literature have largely ignored the presence of women in Kurdish literature. As well as Hassan (2015), another recent study of Kurdish literature from a gendered perspective is: Alhamid L. M. H. (2017) *'You Can't Bury Them All': the Representation of Women in the Contemporary Iraqi Kurdish Novel in Bahdinan.* Unpublished PhD Dissertation. University of Kent.

[5] See Ghaderi and Scalbert Yücel (2021). 'An Etat Présent of the Kurdish Literature in English Translation'. *The Translator.* Only two female poets, Kajal Ahmad and Hiva Pinahi, are

of women in oral Kurdish poetry has been highlighted in some academic studies on Kurdish oral tradition,[6] the role of women in oral literature has been downplayed in literary anthologies in English, often presenting oral poems as 'anonymous'.[7] Such practices are adopted by both Kurdish literary historians, critics, and translators, and have further reinforced the invisibility of women's voices. Nonetheless, balancing their writing practices with other commitments, first and foremost with family life, Kurdish women poets have kept developing their voices while challenging patriarchal traditions and norms of Kurdish society.

The history of classical Kurdish poetry has documented only few female poets. Whilst this phenomenon has social and historical reasons, it must be remembered that our knowledge of classical poetry is limited due to a substantial loss of Kurdish literary heritage as well a significant body of Kurdish written literature remaining unpublished and inaccessible.[8] New studies and publications of Kurdish manuscripts are highly likely to bring to light more female classical poets, as is illustrated in the republication of the *Diwan* of Mestûre Erdelanî (1805–1848) in 2005,[9] which contains her lesser-known Kurdish poems, and more recently the recovery and publication of the *Diwan* of

---

translated at length. See Ahmad, K. (2009). *Poems.* Translation by Mimi Khalvati & Choman Hardi. London: Enitharmon Press and Ahmed, K. (2016). *Handful of Salt.* Translation by Alana Levison Labrosse & Mewan Nahro Said Sofi & Darya Abdul-Karim Ali Najim & Barbara Goldberg. The Word Works. Pinahi is translated into English from Greek: Pinahi, H. (2016) *Secrets of the Snow.* Translated by Zoe Valaoritis (from a Greek translation). Hard Ball Press (place of publication non-identified).

[6] Hassanpour, A. (2014). 'Deng w Rengî Jinan le Hunerî Zarekîda' (women's voice and presence in oral tradition). In Salah Payanyani, *Edebyatî Zarekî Mukriyan: Beşî Jinan* (*Oral Literature of Mukriyan: Women's Part*). Mahabad. On Kurdish oral tradition and women performers, see for instance Schäfers, M. (2018). 'It Used to Be Forbidden': Kurdish Women and the Limits of Gaining Voice. *Journal of Middle East Women's Studies* 14 (1): 3-24; Hamelink, W. (2016). *The Sung Home: Narrative, Morality, and the Kurdish Nation.* Leiden; Boston: Brill.

[7] This is for instance the case in O'Grady, D. (2005). *Kurdish Poems of Love and Liberty.* Mayfield: Agenda.

[8] Ghaderi, F. (2015). 'The Challenges of Writing Kurdish Literary History'. *Kurdish Studies* 3(1): 3-25.

[9] Erdelan, M. (2005). *Dîwanî Mestûre.* M. M. Ruhanî (ed.). Hewlêr: Aras.

Zeyneb Xan (1900–1963), in 2018.[10]

The most celebrated Kurdish female poet in classical poetry is Mah Şeref Xanim Mestûre Erdelan (1805–1848), who was also a historian and a theologian. She is best known for writing *Tarikh-e Ardalan* (*The History of the Ardalans*, 1946), and *Shar'iyat* (2005) which is an instruction book on religious orthodoxy. Both books were composed in Persian. Born in Sanandaj in Western Iran, Mestûre was a member of the nobility in the court of the Ardalan emirate. Mestûre wrote poetry in Persian and in the Gorani dialect of Kurdish. Most of her Kurdish poems, including the one presented in this book, were elegies for her husband, Khosrow Khan, the ruler of the Ardalan principality. Her syllabic metre, her simple diction, and vivid images and metaphors rendered her Kurdish poems accessible, in contrast with her Persian poetry, in which she used strict Arabic scansion (ʿarūż) and Persianate imagery.

In addition to her unique style, differences between her Kurdish and Persian poems represent differences between the Kurdish-Gorani and Persian literary traditions in the nineteenth century. Gorani/Hawrami, the oldest Kurdish literary tradition, was developed between the fifteenth and the nineteenth century under the patronage of the Ardalans in the Persian empire.[11] The personal tone of Mestûre's Kurdish writing sets her apart from her male counterparts and gives her poems a unique feminine quality. Writing in a male dominant context, she was the target of satires as famously illustrated by a *qasida* written by Nalî (1797–1856), renowned Kurdish poet of the nineteenth century and one of the pillars of classical poetry in Sorani. Nalî's satirical poem illustrates the attitude of the mainly male literate and intellectual milieu towards women writers and women's literature. Our recent fieldwork in Duhok in Iraqi Kurdistan (in February 2020, with Yaser Hassan Ali) which aimed to research

[10] Zeyneb Xan (2018). *Dîwan*. Prepared by Hikmet Hemîd Mela. Hewlêr: Rojhelat Publishers.

[11] Ghaderi, F. (2017). 'The Literary Legacy of the Ardalans'. *Kurdish Studies*. 5(1): 32–55.

women's writing practices, revealed that the Kurdish literary milieu has remained patriarchal. Although women writers now have a few strong supporters among the intellectual circle, texts written by women are still generally denigrated and female writers who raise their voices in public are ostracised and often labelled immodest.

With the development of the Kurdish national movement at the end of the nineteenth century and the emergence of Kurdish nationalism, poetry acquired new political significance and developed modern forms as well as new themes. The 'women's question' was one of the new themes related to the themes of progress, modernity, and nationhood. Women's rights were widely discussed, and women's education was advocated by male nationalist poets such as Fayeq Bêkes (1905–1948), and Hêmin (1921–1986). Women's education was part of the Kurdish nationalistic discourse that argued the Kurdish society would not progress until it has educated women, since well-educated women give birth to educated and learned men.[12] Related to the theme of modernisation and progress was also the question of unveiling; veiling was associated with backwardness and unveiling was deemed essential for the advancement of the Kurdish society, thus women were encouraged to unveil by Kurdish poets. As these questions preoccupied the Kurdish intellectuals and literary figures' imagination for the best part of the twentieth century and constitute significant themes in modern poetry, we decided to include two celebrated poems, 'Nasrin' by Fayiq Bêkes,[13] and 'Memory of Shirin' by Hêmin,[14] in this collection to reflect these debates.

Despite the dominance of the 'women's question' in poetry in the early and mid-twentieth century, poetry was largely

---

[12] To read more see Mojab, S. (2001). *Women of a Non-state Nation: the Kurds.* Costa Mesa, Calif.: Mazda Publishers.

[13] The translation was made from the original published in Bêkes, F. (2008). *Dîwanî Fayeq Bêkes.* Çapxaney Şivan.

[14] The translation was made from the original published in Hêmin (2011). *Dîwanî Hêminî Mukriyanî.* Kurdistan.

characterised by male voices and the sidelining of women's voices. Notwithstanding this ongoing trend, in the 1950s in Iraq, women poets such as Pakîze, Xanim, and Xurşîde started to become more prominent by writing, publishing, and contributing to the Kurdish press.[15]

The contexts of the Kurdish uprisings, wars, and violence from the 1960s to the 1990s pushed women further into the private sphere—except for those in guerrilla movements. Composing poetry in Kurdish during these periods was conceived as a political act in itself, focussing largely on resistance and nationalistic themes, leaving no space for women's issues. Kurdish language was banned in Turkey and Syria for decades, therefore writing and publishing in Kurdish was a form of activism and an act of resistance. Poetry and politics were closely interrelated, and poetry was used as a tool to promote political agenda and nationalist ideas, and to express national and collective suffering. Some Kurdish women who took part in the Kurdish political or armed movements started writing in this context. The participation of Kurdish female fighters became prominent with the Komala in Iran and the PKK in Turkey, and more recently in the war against ISIS in Syria and Iraq, where women were at the forefront of the battlefield. A few of these female fighters wrote memoirs, novels, and poems.[16]

While contributing to the nationalistic discourse, female Kurdish poets such as Necîbe Ehmed and Kejal Ehmed, also challenged the patriarchal values. Necîbe Ehmed (born in 1954 in Kirkuk) joined the Peshmerga forces from the late 1981 to the early 1988,[17] and Kejal Ehmed (born in 1967 in Kirkuk) was the

---

[15] Hassan's work dedicates a few sections on this period and authors. Hassan, S. (2015). *Women and Literature: A Feminist Reading of Kurdish Women's Poetry*. Unpublished PhD Dissertation, University of Exeter: 97–99).

[16] The publication house Aram based in Turkey publishes some works produced by women in the guerrilla movement in both Turkish and Kurdish. Recently the memoirs of Sakine Cansiz a prominent founding member of the PKK were translated into English (from German by Janet Biehl). Cansiz, S. (2018). *Sara: My Whole Life Was a Struggle*. London: Pluto Press.

[17]Hassan, S. (2015). *Women and Literature: A Feminist Reading of Kurdish Women's Poetry*. PhD Dissertation, University of Exeter. p. 238.

editor-in-chief of the PUK-owned *Kurdistanî Nwê*. Kejal Ehmed was a distinctive voice and one of the key actors in developing feminist writing and the feminist awakening in Iraqi Kurdistan. From the late 1980s, she developed an original poetic voice using colloquial Kurdish to express women's perspectives and emotions. Her writing was unprecedented in Kurdistan and as such, she encountered strong responses.[18] Similar voices began to develop in Iranian Kurdistan, most notably of Jîla Huseynî.

From the early 1990s, Kurdish female voices could no longer be dismissed and began to be heard in the literary and public spheres in Kurdistan. In the 1990s, the formation of an autonomous Kurdish region and a Kurdish government in Iraq—as well as the lifting of the ban on publication in Kurdish and the rise of pro-Kurdish parties in Turkey—played a crucial role in the revitalisation of Kurdish literature and the emergence of female voices in public life. Kurdish magazines, newspapers, and publishing houses were established in Turkey in the late 1990s and published a few female authors. In the second half of the 2000s, the publishing house Avesta launched "Şahmaran", a collection dedicated to Kurdish female poetry. This literary collection published the works of authors from all parts of Kurdistan, including Fatma Savcı, Lorîn Doğan, Gulîzer, Diya Ciwan, and Kejal Ahmed. Such a collection highlighted, for the first time, the presence of women in Kurdish literature across borders.

Our poetry collection presents samples of both renowned and emerging Kurdish women poets from Iran, Syria, Iraq, and Turkey.

Jîla Huseynî (1964–1996) was born in Saqez, in Iranian Kurdistan. Her formal education was in Persian and like many of her peers in Iran she began her writing career by writing in

---

[18] See Hassan, S. (2015). *Women and Literature: A Feminist Reading of Kurdish Women's Poetry.* PhD Dissertation, University of Exeter. pp.183-191; Ahmed, K. (2016). *Handful of Salt.* Translation by Alana Levison Labrosse & Mewan Nahro Said Sofi & Darya Abdul-Karim Ali Najim & Barbara Goldberg. The Word Works.

Persian. She taught herself Kurdish and her position at the Kurdish Radio Sine (Sanandaj) and meeting and interviewing contemporary Kurdish poets gave her the rare opportunity to develop her writing. Married at the age of fifteen and divorced by twenty, she was well-acquainted with the pains and sufferings of women, which she poignantly depicted in her writing. Her life was tragically cut short in a car accident at the age of thirty-two. Despite her short life, she left a strong legacy that has inspired generations of Kurdish women in Iran. In this collection, we present two of her poems, 'When I Dream About You' and 'Question'. Her writing demonstrates the influence of the developing feminist writing in Iraqi Kurdistan and 'When I Dream About You' is an homage to Necîbe Ehmed.[19]

Diya Ciwan, one of Syrian Kurdistan's most celebrated poets, was born into a religious and intellectual family in Turkish Kurdistan in 1953. After her marriage, she moved to Syria where she started writing in her mother tongue, Kurmanji. She had grown up with the sound of classical poetry recited by her father, and of Kurdish folk stories told by her grandmother. Kurdish folklore has been of great influence on her writing, as has been her love for freedom and her political activism. Her poems, using simple language, celebrate Kurdistan, the struggle of her people, and the love for her country. They also praise the strength of Kurdish women and the hardship they have endured. We present here two poems from her last collection, *Baran* (*Rain*)[20]. In '*Mehboranî* (Pregnancy Craving)', the poet merges themes essential to womanhood —conceiving— to nationalism and the struggle for a homeland. 'The Needle' is a tribute to the tool that has accompanied her throughout her working life. Diya Ciwan worked as a tailoress for forty years, and the needle, her dear tool, enabled her to provide for her family. It also made her

[19] Both poems are taken from first published collection. Jîla Huseynî. (1995). *Geşey Evîn*. Sanandaj: Jiyar publishing.

[20] Diya Ciwan. (2017). *Baran* (*Rain*). Duhok: Xanî Press.

an economically independent woman.

Both Tîroj (born in 1959 in Amêdiyê), and Trîfa Doskî (born in 1974 in Duhok), compose in the Bahdinani dialect of Kurdish, which is spoken in the Bahdinan region of Iraqi Kurdistan. These two poets, despite being well-known in the region, struggled to find a place in the male-dominant literary environment and their conservative society. As a result, both poets adopted pseudonyms. Trîfa's pen name includes her tribe's name, Doskî, which signifies her sense of belonging as well as the weight of patriarchy and family. The use of pen names is extremely current among women poets, both for political reasons and reasons linked to their position as women in society. Gulîzer publishes under her first name only to state her autonomy and sense of universal womanhood. Explaining her decision in a communication with us in September 2020, Gulîzer said, 'I did not want the character of my poetry to be in the shadow of a man, so I have been using a name without a surname because I know that women's words everywhere are quite similar'.

The Bahdinani dialect (a variation of Kurmanji) has been a minority dialect in Iraqi Kurdistan, in which the Sorani dialect dominates. The minority status of Bahdinani explains the strong influence of Arabic in the region, a language that was the main language used in education before the foundation of the Kurdish government. While Trîfa Doskî writes mainly in Bahdinani, Tîroj composes in both Bahdinani and Arabic. Given the oppression of the Kurdish people and their language, Tîroj's use of Arabic has been sometimes criticised by her fellow writers. As a Kurdish writer in Arabic, Tîroj, therefore, struggled to find a place in the literary circles of Kurdistan and Iraq. Today, her work is recognised in the Arabic language haiku movement that developed across Arabic speaking countries. The present collection includes five poems by Doskî.[21] Tîroj's poems

[21] The poems 'A Widow's Hopes' and 'The Bracelet' were published in Doskî, T. (2005). *Êvariyeka Kesk* (*A Green Evening*). 'Symphony' and 'The Beloved, Lost' were published in Doskî,

presented here were written in Arabic in the 1990s and published a decade later in 2007.[22]

Both Tîroj and Doskî's poems echo Kejal Ahmed's works. They daringly explore the themes of love, desire, and sexuality. 'A Widow's Hope' exhibits the effect of violence and war on love relationships, sexuality, and desire. In times of war, for example, it was considered shameful to think of love, and this social shaming perpetuated the subordination of Kurdish women. Violence, however, can also evoke suppressed desires and sexuality and trap women in other relationships of domination. This we can see, for example, in Doskî's 'Cigarette' and 'The Bracelet', and 'Feeling' by Tîroj.

The women poets' direct engagement in themes of sexuality, violence, and gender domination is combined with a reflection on poetry writing, intimacy, and romantic love. Kurdish women poets explore the theme of writing as a place of intimacy, fantasy, and an expression of love and desire. Examples of this can be seen in the poems 'Feeling', 'From the Glow of Imagination', 'Cigarette', and 'The Beloved, Lost'. While Doskî's poems reflect her activism in the field of human rights and women's rights, Tîroj's literary work does not directly embrace the issues of feminism, although she worked with the Women of Kurdistan Union in Duhok between 1993 and 1997.

Viyan Mihemed Tahir, born in 1983 in the village of Dêrîşkê, represents a younger generation of poets in Bahdinan. She started writing and publishing in her mother tongue, Bahdinani Kurdish, in the early 2010s. Her poetry expresses her love for her homeland, and her personal and intimate experiences of womanhood; yet it also reflects and engages with the feelings, sufferings and the pains of her fellow Kurdish women which deeply affect her. Viyan conveys these collective feelings and thoughts through often abstract expressions and complicated

---

T. (2008). *Payîzeka Şîn, (A Blue Autumn)*. Duhok: Ekitiya Niviserên Kurd. The poem 'Falling Apart' is published here for the first time, in both Kurdish and English.

[22] Tîroj (2007). *Wakr al-Khawāter (Nest of Thoughts)*. Duhok.

imageries that, though part of her style, can also be a way to avoid a too strong criticism from a still patriarchal society. Viyan also endeavours to use local words and idioms from her clan, the Berwarî. Her poetry reflects her interest and care for the wealth of Kurdish language, its diversity, and its preservation. We present here two of her poems from her 2020 collection,[23] 'Ego', and 'The Mirror of My Dreams'.

The last poems of this collection are by Gulîzer, born in 1979 in Turkish Kurdistan[24]. Written in Kurmanji Kurdish, Gulîzer's mother-tongue, her poems employ Kurdish proverbs, idioms, and puns, and are deeply embedded in Kurdish oral tradition and folklore. References to storytelling on rooftops, to sewing and dresses, to chests and dowry, weddings and dances, and labour, create a tangible world of Kurdishness and womanhood. Her poetry creates an intimate world, a world of female companionship. But desire and love, pain and separation, loneliness, brokenness, and soothing are never far off.

Feeling deeply constrained and stifled as a woman in a patriarchal society as well as being an oppressed Kurd, Gulîzer uses her poetry in an effort to break free from these constraints. Hence the telling metaphors of sewing, the seamstress, the midwife (a profession she practiced for eight years), and her tools (fabrics, scissors, and stitches to name a few). In the aforementioned September 2020 communication, Gulîzer said: 'I patch my soul with words to make a new dress for myself, to create and give birth to a new self'. Gulîzer's words reflect the relationship of other female writers with the role of poetry in their self-emancipation.[25]

This collection of poems, we hope, is a building block that

---

[23] Mihemed Tahir, V. (2020). *Jinek ji Dûndeha Perperkê* (*A Woman from the Generation of Butterfly*). Duhok.

[24] The poems presented here are all from her latest collection: Gulîzer (2016). *Sindoqa Dirûnê* (*The Sewing Chest*). Istanbul: Avesta.

[25] The special issue of *Kurdish Studies* (issue 6, volume 1, May 2018) edited by Nazand Begikhani, Wendelmoet Hamelink, and Nerina Weiss (2018) on Women and War in Kurdistan, proposes an interesting reflection on the issue of women's resistance and agency. However, not much has been published on women writers and their practices.

will lead to more awareness and recognition of marginalised literary voices, as well as more research on Kurdish women writers and translation of their works.

Mestûre Erdelan

Mah Şeref Xanim Mestûre Erdelan (1805–1848) is celebrated Kurdish writer, poet, and historian. She was born in Sanandaj in Iranian Kurdistan and died in exile in Sulaymaniyah. Mestûre was the second wife of Khosrow Khan of Ardalan, the ruler of the Ardalan principality. She studied Arabic and Persian and wrote poetry in Persian and the Kurdish dialect of Gorani/Hawrami. Besides her poetry, she is known for her *Tarikh-e Ardalan* (*The History of the Ardalans*) and *'Aqayed* a book of religious instructions, both written in Persian. While her Persian poetry is the prototype of Persian poetry of the nineteenth century, she followed the Gorani literary tradition in her Kurdish writing. Her elegies for her husband, Khosrow Khan, are among the most renowned elegies in Kurdish poetry.

خەسرەوم وەهار

خەسرەوم وەهار، خەسرەوم وەهار
یاشا نەیەوە ئیمساڵ نەوەهار
بەرنەیان وە بەر گوڵان جە گوڵزار
نەکەرۆ درەخت شکۆفە ئیزهار
نە سەحنی چەمەن نەوانۆ بولبول
هەنی نەکێشۆ ژاڵە نە ڕووی گوڵ
نیلوفەر تا حەشر بەرنەیۆ جە ئاو
جە ڕووی گوڵی سورخ نەکێشۆ گوڵاو
بەنەفشە و سونبول نەسرین و شەوبۆ
تا قامی قیام بەرنەیان جە کۆ
سۆسەن و لالە و ڕەعنا و گوڵە زەرد
هەنی سەوز نەبان چەنی سۆز و دەرد
سوپای گوڵاڵان خوار و نگون بۆ
شەقایق ڕەنگ زەرد، جگەر پڕ هوون بۆ

An Elegy for Khosrow

My Khosrow, spring is here;
how I wish it would not have come this year,
that no sprouts would have sprung in the garden,
no trees would have come into buds,
no nightingale in the meadow,
no dew on the petals.
How I wish water lilies did not bloom until Doomsday
and no rosewater was steeped;
that violets, wallflowers, and hyacinths never push out of the ground again;
that tulips, lilies, yellow flowers, and basil
would not spring forth my pain.
How I wish the throngs of blossoms would be destroyed
and poppies would yellow with aching hearts.

Translator: Farangis Ghaderi
Translation editor: Rinat Harel

Hêmin

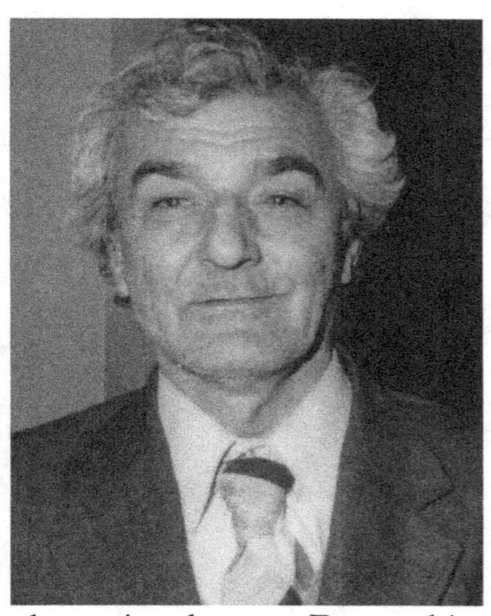

Hêmin (1921–1986) was the pen name of the acclaimed Kurdish poet, writer, and translator, Seyed Mohammad Amin Shaikholislami Mukri. He was born in the village of Lachin, near Mahabad in 1921. In 1942, he joined Komeley Jiyanewey Kurd (The Kurdish Resurrection Society), where he adopted his pseudonym. In the Republic of Mahabad in 1946, he was named as one of the national poets. Due to his political activism, he took refuge in Iraqi Kurdistan in 1968 and settled in Baghdad in 1970. He returned to Iran after the fall of the Pahlavi regime in 1979, quit politics, and set up the Salah al-Din Ayubi Kurdish publishing house and established the Kurdish journal *Sirwe* (*The Morning Breeze*), serving as its editor until his death in 1986. *Sirwe* gave young Kurdish writers and poets a space to publish and share their works and was instrumental in the development of modern Kurdish literature in Iran. Hêmin is one of the most loved poets in Iranian and Iraqi Kurdistan, and parents continue to name their children after him. His most famous poetry collections are *Tarîk û Rûn* (*Dark and Twilight*) and *Nalley Cudayî* (*Laments of Separation*). He was an ardent advocate of women's education and 'liberation', which he argued are essential for the 'progress' of the Kurdish society.

یادگاری شیرن

چاوەکەم! چاوی ڕەشی تۆ ئافەتی گیانی منە
گیانەکەم! برژانگی تیژت نووکە ڕمبی دوژمنە

شیری دەستی شێری ئاڵایە برۆ ڕاکشاوەکەت
جەرگی لاوێکی هەژاری کوردی ورد پێ بنجنە

دیدەکەی بەخوماری تۆ تورکانە بەدمەستی دەکا
بۆیە مەیلی وا بە کێشە و فیتنە و خوێن ڕشتنە

بەژنەکەت سێدارەیە، کەزیەت تەنافە زوو بە دەی
بیخە ئەستۆی من کە کوردم، کورد بەشی خنکاندنە

زامی جەرگی من بە فەرموودەی گراوی سواری کورد
مەلهەمی هەر ژەنگی گوارە و ئارەقی بەر گەردنە

ئارەزوومە هیچ نەبێ جارێکی ماچ کەم زاری تۆ
ئارەزوی من چووکە، ئەمما تا بفەرمووی شیرنە

دڵ بە گرمەی تۆپی گەورەی دوژمنیش ڕانەچڵەکێ
دادەخورپێ ئەم دڵە ئەمما بە خرمەی بازنە

خەڵکی دنیا ڕازی دڵداری بە «بێتەل» پێک دەڵێن
ڕاسپاردەی لاو و کیژی کوردە ئێستاکەش شنە

ڕۆژی بەختی هەر لە ژێر هەورێکی ڕەشدا لاوی کورد
تاکوو ڕوخساری کچی شاری لە پێش چاوان ونە

نایەلێ گۆشەی برۆکەت دەرکەوێ چارشێوەکەت
ئەی لەدەس ئەو چلکە هەورە مانیعی مانگ گرتنە

Memory of Shirin

Your dark eyes, my darling, plague my body.
Your sharp eyelashes, my soul, are the enemy's spearheads.

Your eyebrow is the sword held in the Lion's Hand.
With it, a poor Kurdish lad's heart is finely chopped.

Your drowsy eyes are like a drunkard Turk,
plotting and shedding blood.

Your body is the gallows, your braid, the hanging rope.
Come, wrap it around my Kurdish neck. Hanging is the Kurd's fate.

The earrings' rust and the cleavage's sweat-beads,
a Kurdish horseman said, will remedy my wounded heart.

I wish to kiss your mouth this once.
My wish is small, but oh, so sweet.

My Heart is not startled by the enemy's heavy shelling,
yet it races at the mere sound of jingling bangles.

Elsewhere, lovers' words are whispered down the phone;
here, they are borne on the wind.

So long as the girls' faces are covered,
the sun of the Kurdish lad is clouded over.

Your *charshew* veils the edge of your eyebrow.
That hideous cloud eclipses the moon of your face.

چۆن دەبێ سەربەست گەلی ژێردەست کە کچ دابەستە بێ؟
بەس نەبێ ئەو کۆیلەتی و ئەو کچ لە ژوور دابەستنە؟!

دەرکی داخستوە لە تۆ بابت کەچی دەرکی نییە
دەرکە داخستن لە تۆ دەرکی هومێد داخستنە

دارزینە، مردنە، ئاخر هەتا کەی پێت بڵێن
نابێ بێتە دەر لە ماڵ، مافی ژیانی کوا؟ ژنە

لادە چارشێوی ڕەشت با دەرکەوێ کوڵمەی گەشت
چون لە قەرنی بیستەما زۆر عەیبە ئەو ڕوو گرتنە

کیژی خەڵکی بۆمی ئاتۆمی دروست کرد و ئەتۆش
هەردەزانی ناوی «ئەستێوڵک» و «دەرخۆنە» و «پنە»

فێری زانست و هونەر بوو ئەو لەسایەی خوێندنی
تۆش تەشیمان بۆ دەڕێسی، یادگاری شیرنە

ئەو بە ئاسمانا فڕی، دنیا گەڕا، چوە بن بەحر
دەک نەمێنم کاری ئێوەش هەر لە ژوور دانیشتنە

کوڕ بەزێنە ئەو لە عیلم و ئەو لە کار و سەنعەتا
گۆرەویشە سەنعەتی تۆ، پێت خەنی بووم بیچنە

ئەو پەچە و ڕووبەند و چارشێوەی نەدیوە نەنکی تۆ
ئەو شڕ و شاڵاتە دیاری دوژمنی دڵ چڵکنە

کیژی شێخ و کیژی حاجی و کیژی ئاغا ڕەنجەڕۆن
کیژی ئازادە ئەوی ژینی بە نووکی گاسنە

شەنگەبێری یار و دەسباری کوڕی کۆچەر نەبێ
چۆن دەگاتە جێ هەوار و هۆبە ئەو بارگە و بنە؟

How could the oppressed be free when the women are chained?
Enough to slavery, enough to keeping women indoors.

By shutting the door on you, your ignorant father
has shut the door on Hope.

It is a shame you are told to not leave the house!
What is her right to live? She's a woman!

Peel back your dark *charshew*—show your rosy cheeks.
Veiling is shameful in the 20th century!

Other nations' daughters invented the Atomic Bomb, and you
only know your breadboard, and the clay pot.

She was educated in science and art,
and you spend your days spinning yarn, keeping Shirin's memory.

She flew across the sky, went around the world, dove into the sea.
Alas, your days are spent at home.

She surpasses men in science, work, and industry.
Knitting is your industry; keep on knitting, you make me oh, so proud!

Your grandmother did not see this Veiling.
These rags are the enemy's gift to us!

While the daughters of Sheikhs, Hajjis, and Aghas are kept indoors,
the free girls are ploughing the fields.

How could the grazing cattle and the shepherds reach their summer pastures without the cowgirls?

قەڵشی دەست و کوڵمی سووتاوی کچی لادێ نەبێ
چۆن دەگاتە دەستی دەسبڕ ئەو هەموو تاتووتنە؟

نیسک و نۆک و ماشی ناو عەمباری ئاغای مفتەخۆر
پاک لەسایەی دەسکەنەی «زین» و «مرۆت» و «سۆسنە»

شۆڕەژن بنکۆڵ نەکا بڕکەی بە قرچەی نیوەڕۆ
چۆن لە کاڵەک تێر دەبێ ئەو زگ زلە بێستان ڕنە؟

کوا مەتاعی کوردەواریمان دەچوو بۆ هەندەران؟
گەر بە سەربەستی نەژیبا ئەو کچە مازووچنە

بێر و هاوێری لەگەڵ کاکی نەکردبا بن پشک
چۆن دەمانبوو ئەو هەموو گۆشت و پەنیر و بەرگنە؟

دەست و کەرکیتی کچی نازداری هەوشاری نەبا
چۆن دەڕازاوە بەقاڵی شار و بازاڕی سنە؟

با هەزار (زێ) و (گادەر) و(لاوێنی) ڕوونیشمان هەبێ
تاکوو ژن ئازاد نەبێ، سەرچاوەکەی ژین لیخنە

کۆیلەتی باوی نەماوە، کیژی کوردی خۆشەویست!
ڕاپەڕە، هەستە لە خەو، ئاخر چ وەختی خەوتنە؟

دەرکە بشکێنە، پەچە بدڕێنە، ڕاکە مەدرەسە
چاری دەردی کوردەواری خوێندنە، هەر خوێندنە

دایکی زانایە کوڕی ئازا دەنێرێتە خەبات
من گوتم تۆش تێبگە: «ناگاتە دەریایە زنە»

گوارەکەی زێڕت بەکار نایە، لەگوێ بگرە قسەم
لایقی گوێی تۆ عەزیزم شێعری سادەی «هێمنە»

How could sacks of tobacco reach the exploitive merchants
if not for these girls' callused palms and sunburnt faces?

Black lentils and chickpeas are stored in the barn of the freeloading landlord, harvested from thorny plants by village girls like Zên, Mirot, and Siwêsin.

If not for the capable farming girl's toil in the high noon heat,
how could the patron's potbelly be filled with melon?

How could Kurdish goods reach foreign lands
if the harvesting girls did not live freely?

If the village girl did not accompany her brother to the grazing pastures, how could we have all that cheese and meat?

How could Sine and its markets be adorned with carpets
if not for the sweet hands of Hawshar's weaving-girls?

Even if we have thousands of clear-watered rivers like Zê, Gader, and Lawên, life's springs will muddy if women are not free.

Slavery is outdated, dear Kurdish girl!
Rise, awaken—it is not the time to sleep!

Break the door, rip the veil, run to school.
The remedy for the Kurdish malady is education, education.

It is the educated mother who sends her brave son to the battlefield.
I tell you: the pond can never reach the sea.

Your golden earrings have no use; take my words instead.
Your ears, my darling, deserve Hêmin's simple poems.

Translator: Farangis Ghaderi
Translation editor: Rinat Harel

Fayeq Bêkes

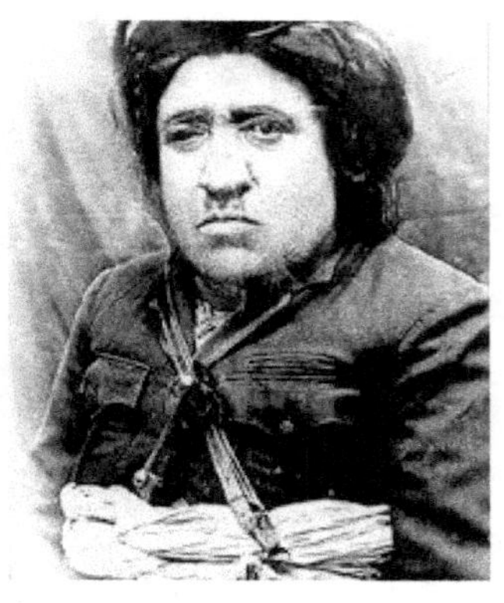

Fayeq Bêkes (1905-1948) was one of the most iconic Kurdish nationalist poets of the twentieth century. He was born in the village of Sîtek, near Sulaymaniyah, and his childhood was marked by tragedies and the losses of his parents. Enduring the life of an orphan, poverty, and exile later in his life due to his political activities led him to adopt the pen name 'Bêkes' (Forsaken). His nationalistic poems and his anticolonial stance has been inspirational for generations of Kurdish intellectuals. He is also celebrated as one of the most passionate advocates of women's education and he encouraged unveiling. He was the father of the legendary Kurdish poet, Şêrko Bêkes.

نەسرین

نەسرین دەمێکە داخت لە دڵمە
گیرۆدەی بەندی، ژیانت زوڵمە
وا من پێت ئەڵێم چونکە لە سەرمە
هەستە تێکۆشە تا خوێنت گەرمە
سەرپۆش فڕێ دە چ وادەی شەرمە

ئەمڕۆ زەمانی عیلم و عیرفانە
عالەم شەو و ڕۆژ وا لە فرمانە
فەرقی نێر و مێ نییە بیزانە
هەستە تێکۆشە تا خوێنت گەرمە
سەرپۆش فڕێ دە چ وادەی شەرمە

مەڵێ من کچم، تۆش وەکو منی
موحتاجی عیلم و فەن و خوێندنی
مەجبووری ئیش و خزمەت کردنی
هەستە تێکۆشە تا خوێنت گەرمە
سەرپۆش فڕێ دە چ وادەی شەرمە

هێندە دانیشتی پشتت چەماوە
زەرد و لاواز بوویت هێزت نەماوە
کچی بێگانەت خۆ لە بەرچاوە
هەستە تێکۆشە تا خوێنت گەرمە
سەرپۆش فڕێ دە چ وادەی شەرمە

Nasrin

Nasrin, it has been a long time that my heart burns for you;
you are chained, your life is oppression-filled.
I tell you, it is my duty to do so:
Rise, endeavour, until your blood is warm.
Throw away the veil, there's no shame in that.

Now is the age of science, and knowledge,
People of the world toil day and night.
Realise, there's not difference between men and woman.
Rise, endeavour, until your blood is warm.
Throw away the veil, there's no shame in that.

Don't say, "I am a woman"- like me,
you need knowledge, skill, and education.
You have to work and serve.
Rise, endeavour, until your blood is warm.
Throw away the veil, there's no shame in that.

You sat for so long, your back turned hunched.
You are pale, thin, and worn-out.
Can't you see the foreign girls?
Rise, endeavour, until your blood is warm.
Throw away the veil, there's no shame in that.

خشڵ و جوانی تۆ حەیا و فێربوونە
پاشەڕۆژیشت هەر بەوان ڕوونە
کچی بێ عیلم دیل و زەبوونە
هەستە تێکۆشە تا خوێنت گەرمە
سەرپۆش فڕێ دە چ وادەی شەرمە

وەك خۆشك و برا ئەبێ هەر دووکمان
قۆڵی لێ هەڵکەین بچینە مەیدان
تا کورد بەرینە ریزی میللەتان
هەستە تێکۆشە تا خوێنت گەرمە
سەرپۆش فڕێ دە چ وادەی شەرمە

سلێمانی، ١٩٤٤

Your beauty and jewels are modesty and learning;
your bright future depends on them.
A woman with no knowledge is chained and wretched.
Rise, endeavour, until your blood is warm.
Throw away the veil, there's no shame in that.

Like brother and sister, both of us should
roll up our sleeves, head to the battlefield,
and elevate the Kurds to the height of other nations.
Rise, endeavour, until your blood is warm.
Throw away the veil, there's no shame in that.

Silêmanî, 1944

Translator: Farangis Ghaderi
Translation editor: Rinat Harel

Jîla Huseynî

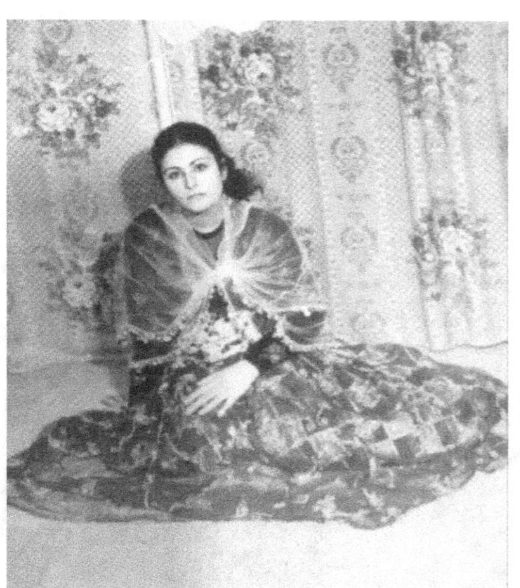

Jîla Huseynî was born in 1964 in Saqez, in Iran. Like many of her peers in Iran, she began her writing career by writing in Persian and taught herself Kurdish. Her position at the Radio Sine (Sanandaj) gave her the opportunity to further develop her writing. She published her poems in literary journals and magazines such as *Sirwe*, and her first poetry collection entitled *Geşey Evîn* (*The Blooming of Love*) was published in 1995. Her life was tragically cut short in a car accident at the age of thirty-two when she was on her way to meet the legendary Kurdish poet, Şêrko Bêkes. Her dîwan, *Qalay Raz (The Fortress of Mystery),* was published posthumously in 1999 in three parts and included her Kurdish and Persian poems and her short stories.

كە خەو بە تۆوە ئەبینم

(١)

خەو ئەبینم
دەستم ئەگری و لە تۆفانی سەرسامیدا
بەرەو کەنار ئەمرفێنی
بۆ بەیانی ....
خۆت تۆفانی

(٢)

لە خەوما تۆ
کورە باڵا بەرزەکەیت و
دەس هەڵئەبڕی
لە باخەکەی دراوسێتان
سێوێک ئەدزی و ئەیدەی بە من
دائەچڵەکێم
باخەوانێکی تووڕەیت و
سێوەکەت لێ دائەشارم.

(٣)

هەرچی شەوە تۆ پاڵەوانی خەوەکان
تۆ ئەستێرە و شاخ و ئاسمان
جوانی و بزە و مێهرەبانی ....
بۆ بەیانی؟!

پێشکەشە بە کورتە شیعرەکانی خانمی نەجیبە ئەحمەد بە نێوی "وردە گلەیی"

When I Dream About You

(1)

I dream that
you take my hand and in a storm of turmoil
rush me to the shore.
In the morning
you are the storm itself.

(2)

In my dream, you
are the handsome boy
who stole an apple from the neighbour's grove
for me.
I wake up.
You are an angry gardener and
I hide away the apple.

(3)

Each night, you are the hero of my dreams.
You are the star, the mountain, the sky.
You are beauty, smile, and kindness...
In the morning?!

* Dedicated to Ms Najiba Ahmad's poetry collection, *Usual Gripes*

Translator: Farangis Ghaderi
Translation Editor: Rinat Harel

پرسیار

سەرپۆشە شڕەکەی دایکم

دەس بەرداری سەرم نابێ و

ئەڵێ: "من هی داپیرەتم"

ڕەنگە ئەویش لە داپیرەی خۆیەوە بۆی بەجێ مابێ

سەریشم پەنجەرەی تاقبازی بەرەو ئاسمانە

حەز ئەکا ڕۆژان میوانداری هەتاو بکات و

شەوانیش مانگ و ئەستێرە.

چاویلکەیەکی قەترانیش لەدایکم بۆ ماوەتەوە

ئەڵێ: "دنیا هەر ئەمەیە تۆ ئەیبینی"

لە گەڵ هەر گرمەی هەورێکا، قارچکی سەد پرسیاری

دووپات و تازەش

لە چاوانما هەڵئەتۆقێت.

Question

My mother's worn scarf
does not leave my head alone.
It says: 'I am your grandmother's'.
It might have been her grandmother's too.
And my head is an open window to the sky,
wishing to host the sun at day
and the moon and the stars at night.
My mother also left a pair of pitch-black glasses.
It says: 'This is the world as you see it'.
With every thunderclap, a mushroom of a hundred questions
old and new sprout in my eyes.

Translator: Farangis Ghaderi
Translation editor: Rinat Harel

Diya Ciwan

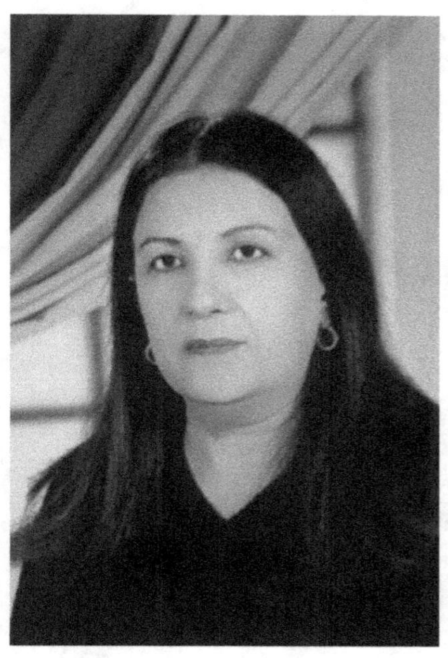

Diya Ciwan is one of Syrian Kurdistan's most celebrated poets. She was born into a religious and intellectual family in Turkish Kurdistan in 1953. She married in Qamishli and moved with her family to Damascus in 1975. Her home became well-known for artistic and intellectual activities, and she started writing poetry in Kurdish in 1977. To support her family, she worked as a tailoress for forty years. But she has also always been politically active. She has been residing in Iraqi Kurdistan since 2012 where she has taken on an important role in the central committee of the Kurdistan Democratic Party–Syria. She is also a member of the Committee of Supporting Syrian Women's Issues. Diya Ciwan published nearly ten books in Kurdish, including short-stories, folklore, and poetry. Her first poetry collection *Pêlek ji Derya Kovanên Min* (*A Wave of Sea of My Sorrows*) was published in Damascus in 1992, and her last collection *Baran* (*Rain*) was published in Duhok in 2017. Her poems are translated into Arabic, Turkish, and Russian.

Derzî

Vê derziyê çi kiriye û çi nekiriye
Bi vî qelafetê piçûk karê gêsinekî kiriye
Min bi serê wê yê zirav devê birçîbûnê dirût û
Xizanî bingor kiriye
Çekê min ê giran ew e
Ji xencerekî tûjtir e
Ji hemî gotinên qelew jêhatir û kêrhatîtir e
Her ko di nav destê min de diçilwile
Xwîna di bin neynokê bi wê şêrîntir e
Dema derdorê vî cawî nîgar dike
Deşt û beyarên jiyanê tev cot dike
Bi bejna wê her ez çavê xwe kil dikim
Bi kuriya wê stûna jiyanê hildidim
Ko carekê ji min winda dibe
Bi hewarî lê digerim
Ta ko ronî ji çav negere
Ji wê nagerim
Ez tu carî wê bi şûrê Şamê naguherim.

The Needle

So much, this needle has done!
With her tiny body, she did the work of a ploughshare.
With her delicate tip, I sewed shut
the mouth of hunger,
and buried destitution.
She's my heavy weapon,
sharper than a dagger,
handier than big words.
When she gleams in my hand
the blood under my fingernail turns sweet.
On my fabric
she ploughs the plains and the fallow land of life.
With her shaft, I kohl my eyes.
With her sharp end, I raise the pillar of life.
If she drops out of sight
I shall look for her, crying for help.
For as long as there is light in my eyes
I shall never leave her,
or swap her for the Sword of Damascus.

Translator: Clémence Scalbert Yücel
Translation editor: Rinat Harel

Mehboranî

Dema pîrek
Mehboraniya dikin …
Dilê wan dibije
Tirş û şûr û şêrîn
Lê dema
Dayika min
Mehboranî dikirin
Dilê wê dibijiya
Axa sor

Mehboranî: rewşa jinên ducan in ko dilê wan dice tiştan. Dilê her jinekê dibije tiştekê taybet.

Mehboranî (Pregnancy Craving)

Pregnant women
crave salty, sour, and sweet.
But my mum
craved
Red Soil.

Translator: Clémence Scalbert Yücel
Translation editor: Rinat Harel

Tîroj

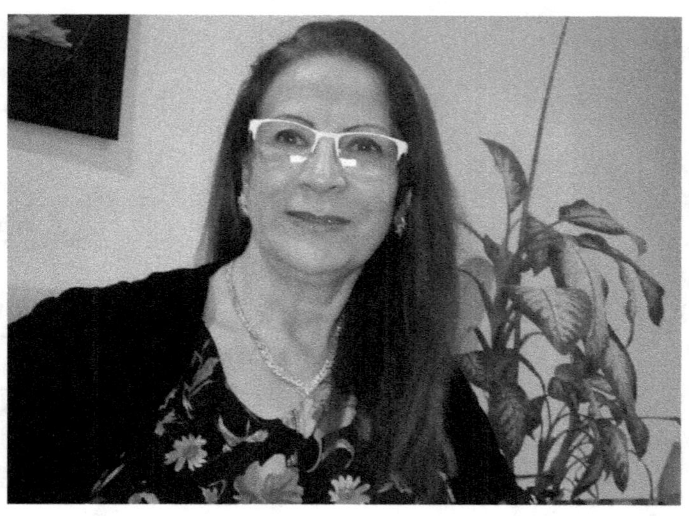

Tîroj (or Tîroj Amêdî) is the pseudonym of the Kurdish poet Hana Mohamed, who writes in both Arabic and Kurdish. She was born in 1959 in Amêdiyê, Iraqi Kurdistan, and spent some of her childhood years in the south of Iraq. She graduated from the Teachers' Training Institute in Duhok in 1978, and worked as a teacher for many years. Tîroj started publishing her poetry in Arabic in *Khabāt* newspaper and *Māf* magazine in the mid 1990s. She later learned to write in Kurdish, her mother tongue. Her poetry collections include *Wakr al-Khawāter* (*Nest of Thoughts*, 2007) in Arabic, *Şiyan û Leylan* (*Ability and Mirage*, 2002) and *Perê Spî* (*White Paper*, 2012) in Kurdish. Her collections of haikus and tankas in Arabic include *Areej al-Banafsaj* (*Fragrant Violets*, 2020) and *Thawrat al-Matar* (*Rain of Revolution*, 2020). A member of the Union of Kurdish Writers, Tîroj is currently preparing her new collection of haikus written in Kurdish to be published in 2021.

من وَهجِ الخيال

في خاطري..
بين جُمل أشعاري
نثرتُ حروف اسمكَ
فكانت شذى وبلسما..
رأيتُ نفسي
سحابة ومرتْ
في زرقة سماء
ولم تقطر
رذاذاً أو مطر..
كسرتُ قلمي
مزّقتُ أوراقي
حرقتها
لأنَّ الحُبَّ
لم يُخلق لي...

From the Glow of Imagination

In my mind's eye
Between the lines of my poetry
The letters of your name are scattered
Fragrant like a sweet-smelling balm
I saw myself
Like a passing cloud
In the blue of the sky
From which not a single drop would fall
I broke my pen
I tore up my pages
And set them on fire
Because love
Is not meant for me…

Co-translators: Mohammed Asiri, Christina Phillips, Lara Radusin, Daisy Vaughan

عاطفة

بأيّ اسمٍ أناديك؟!
قيودٌ وأساورٌ تكبّلني
من رأسي لأخمصِ قدمي
خذ الاسمَ
من نبرةِ صوتي
من عبرتي
من رجفة يدٍ
ترنو إليك
خذ نبضي من حمرة وجنتي
من خجلي وارتباكي
بتمردي آخذ ثأري
إحساسٌ يؤرقني
في ثورتي وانتقامي
ببريق عينيَّ أسترسلُ
وأملّيكَ كلامي

Feeling

What do I call you?
Chains and shackles
from head to toe.
The word
lies in the tone of my voice,
in my tears,
in my trembling hands.
Craving you.
See my pulse, my flushed cheeks
in shyness and confusion.
My rebellion is vengeance.
Insomnia.
Our revolt our revolution
and I will follow the light.
Mark my words.

Co-translators: Mohammed Asiri, Christina Phillips, Lara Radusin, Daisy Vaughan

Trîfa Doskî

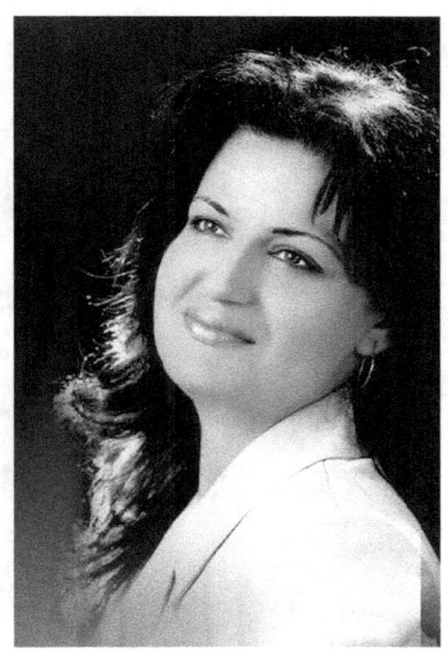

The poet and writer Trîfa Doskî was born in 1974 in Duhok, Iraqi Kurdistan. She received her diploma in Arabic Language (1996) in Duhok and began publishing her poetry and articles in the mid 1990s in Kurdish newspapers and magazines. At that time, she also worked for NGOs in Iraqi Kurdistan. She published three poem collections in Bahdinani Kurdish: *Straneka Spî (A White Song)* in 2000, *Êvariyeka Kesk (A Green Evening)* in 2005, and *Payizeka Şîn (A Blue Autumn)* in 2008. An active member of the Union of Kurdish Writers, Doskî had her poems translated into Arabic, and is well-known as a daring feminist writer and an activist for gender equality.

ئەز و بازن

من دکەی بویك

و هەناسا من دوورپێچ دکەی

د کەڤلوژانەکێ پۆسیدە دا هزار خەون درزن

حەزێن من د سینگێ بارانێ دا دنڤن

ژیێ چاڤێن من دو رۆژ بوون

تە تەلیەك نیشا من دا

ئاوری و گول و هۆزانێن من

تەلی دهێنە د رێکێ دا

تەلیەك

دو تەلی

سێ تەلی

سەد تەلی..

من بدەنە دەستێ بای.. دا سترانەکا نەرم بۆ من بێژیتن..

من ببەنە پێش وێ کچا رویس دلەیزیتن دا خۆ بنیاسم

دەمار دشدیێن

بازن تەنگ بوو

بازن تەنگتر لێهات

بتنێ من دەنگێ مای، گونەها من نینە ئەز کچم....

The Bracelet

You make me a bride
and you encircle my breath …
In a wilted shell a thousand dreams decay.

My desires sleep in the bosom of the rain.
My eyes were two days old,
you showed me a snare.
My gaze, my flowers, my poems;
snares are placed in their way …
One snare
Two snares
Three snares
A hundred snares …
Give me to the hand of the wind… so it may sing me a soft song …
Take me to that naked dancing girl, so I may know myself.

The blood boils,
the bracelet has tightened,
the bracelet tightens ever more.
Only my voice remains; it is not my sin I am a girl …

Co-translators: Yaser Hassan Ali, Yunus Abakay, Christine Robins, Clémence Scalbert Yücel
Translation editor: Rinat Harel

سمفۆنی

١

دو شعرێن سپی خۆ د ناڤ پەرتۆکەکێ دا بزر کربوو

دەما پەرتۆك هاتیە ڤەکرن

شعر مینا دو کچێن سنێلە سۆر سۆر بوون.

٢

(جگارە)

من ژ ناڤتەنگێ را دگری

وەك جگارێ

دکێشیە ناڤا خۆ

دمێژی

دهەلمێژی

و دهەلکێشی

سپێدێ د خمخمکێن ژۆرا خۆ دا بەرددەیە بای.

٣

ژنەکا روهنم وەك بەلگێن روحانەکێ

د رۆمانێن تە دا

د شعرێن تە دا

کلیلا باژاری ددەمە دەستێ تە

و بلا پەرتۆك ل سەر دەستێ تە پاکیزەییا خۆ ژ دەست بدەن

پەرتۆکێ رویس بکە

ژ حەرفان و بکە مەی

بدە چویچکا، دا سەمایەکا تژی شەهوەت بکەن

Symphony

1
Hidden, two white poems
blushed red like two teenage girls
when the book opened.

2 (cigarette)
You hold me by the waist
Like a cigarette
You inhale me
You suck me in
You suck me all in
You fill your lungs.
Come morning, you exhale me out of the nostrils of your room
to the wind.

3
I am a translucent woman like basil's leaves
in your novels
and in your poems
I hand you the key of the city
So the book may lose its purity in your hands.
Undress the book from its letters,
turn it into wine,
give it to the birds, so they can dance full of desire.

٤

ژ ترسێن نەهاتنا تە

چ شعر ژ سەرێ من دەرنەکەتن

د مالێ دا مات ببوون

ل بەندا چاڤێ تە بوون

تو هاتی

شعرەك بهاری خۆ ل بەر من را دهلاڤێت دڤیا بچیتە کۆلانێن دلێ تە

٥

ئاڤەکا هناری مە

بەرددەمە سەر لێڤێن تە تو دین دبی

دبیە گورگ

تە هشك دکەم

دبیە گورگ

چەوا تە ژ خۆ ڤەکەم؟

4.
Fearing that you wouldn't come,
no poems sprang out of my head;
they were at home, lifeless
waiting for your eyes.
You came,
a springtime poem bounced around me,
eager to find its way to the streets of your heart.

5
I am pomegranate juice.
I pour myself on your lips, you turn crazy.
You become a wolf.
I dry you out.
You're still a wolf.
How do I get you off of me?

Co-translators: Yaser Hassan Ali, Yunus Abakay, Christine Robins, Clémence Scalbert Yücel
Translation editor: Rinat Harel

هیڤیێن بێوەژنەکێ

ئێدی حەز ناکەم باسی شەری بکەم
و کەلەخێ وەلاتی ل ناڤ ریپۆرتاژەکا سۆتی دا ببینم
تو ل ناڤ تەرمان دا ب من دگرنژی
سەحکە دوماهیکا چیرۆکا مە دگەل دەمی
سالا ١٩٨٨ێ بویك و زاڤا بووین
ژ چاڤێن تە ئەوێن پاشایان کرینە سەنگەر و تێدا وەلات
چکلاندی
من شەرم دکر بێژم
حەژ تە دکەم
من نەگۆت.. نەگەهشتم بێژم
تاکو شەرما خۆ من کریە بەرەك و هاڤێتی
تو ل بەر چاڤێن من نەمای
ئەڤرۆ یا بوویە دەفتەرەك و ئەز د ناڤ لاپەرێن وێ دا
وەك ماسیەکێ ب هشکی خۆ دگەڤێزم
ئەز گەلەك هەوجەی تەمە
شازدە سالە ل بەر دەرگەهێ مێژوویێ مە ناهێلن بچمە ژۆر
شازدە سالە هەسپێ تە بەرەف زۆزانا رەڤی و دگەل
سیارەکێ بیانی بووینە هەڤال
شازدە سالە من دڤێت تو بهێی دا بێژمە تە
ئێدی شەرم ناکەم.. حەژ تە دکەم.. حەژ تە دکەم..
حەژ تە دکەم

A Widow's Hopes

From now on, I do not want to talk about war
nor see the corpse of my homeland in a charred newspaper.
From amongst the dead, you smile at me.
Look at the end of our story through time:

In the year 1988, we were bride and groom.
The pashas turned your eyes into a trench, jabbing
the homeland in them.
I was ashamed to say
I love you.
I did not say it … I missed my chance.
By the time I had made my shame into a stone and thrown it,
you were out of sight.

Today has become a notebook, and in its pages I flounder
like a fish out of water.
I need you so much.

Refused entry, I have been standing at the gate of history for sixteen
years.
Your horse escaped to the highland pastures and befriended
a foreign rider sixteen years ago.
For sixteen years, I have wanted you to come so I can tell you
that now, I'm no longer ashamed … I love you … love you…
love you.

ناسنامه گوهارتن

ناڤ: شەرمین

ژی: ٣٠ سال

بارێ کەسایەتی: بێوەژن

ئێدی شەرمە.. گولا بۆ خۆ بکەمە قەفتك

و هەموو بوهاران بکەمە رووبارەکێ گەرم

و شەرمە پرچا خۆ بۆ رۆژێ خەنا کەم

ئەز سفرم ل راستا ژمارا

وەلات بوویە گۆرستانەکا ب کۆم

و هەر بهوستەکا پێ خۆ ددانمێ، هزر دکەم سەرێ تە

ئەوێ ل سەر زەندا من دخەوچوو یێ نفستیە

لەورا دڤەجنقم

پاشڤە دچم نەوێرم بچم

وەرە بێژە تو ل کیڤە ل هێڤیا منی دا بێم

They changed her identity.
Name: Şermîn.
Age: 30 years old.
Marital status: widow.
Now it is shameful … to make a crown of flowers for myself,
and to turn into a hot river every spring.
And it is shameful to henna my hair for the sun.
Now, I am nought.
The homeland has become a mass grave,
and I cannot put down my foot anywhere, I fear I'll step
on your head; oh, you who once slept in my arms.
So I panic.
I step back and I do not dare walk forward.
Come, tell me where you wait for me, so I can join you.

Co-translators: Yaser Hassan Ali and Clémence Scalbert Yücel
Translation editor: Rinat Harel

حەیران و بەرزەبوون

تو دبێژی ئەڤ چەند سالە ئەم ل هەڤ دگەرن؟ مە چەند جارا یاری ل کۆلانێن تەنگ و
تاری دکرن
پێنجۆکانێ و دامانێ
ئەز ل پشت تە بووم تە نەددیتم.. سیتافکا تە من نڤاند.
هزار سالە ئەز دەستێن تە ل سەر برینێن خۆ ددانم و تو دبێژی کا تو؟
ل کۆلانێن هەلبەستا تە شین تبلێن من هەنە، ل زنارێن پەرتۆکێن تە دەوسا کوترا و
پەلاتینکێن من هەنە. دناڤ رۆمانێن تە دا
قەهرەمانێن من هاتنە ئەنفالکرن و بێوەژنێن من شـــویکرینە و پرچ خەنا کرینە. پەرتۆکێن
تە چەند شرین د هەمبێزا خۆ دا
دگڤێشم

The Beloved, Lost

Do you know how many years we've been looking for each other?
How many times we've played in dark and narrow streets?
Games of Fivestones and Checkers.
I was behind you, you didn't see me … I put your shadow to sleep.
For a thousand years I put your hand on my wounds, but still you ask, where are you?
My fingerprints are all over the streets of your poem; the imprints of your doves and butterflies all over the cliffs of your books. In your novels, my protagonists have been massacred in the *Anfal;* my widows have been married, their hair is hennaed. How sweetly I embrace your books.

Co-translators: Yaser Hassan Ali and Clémence Scalbert Yücel
Translation editor: Rinat Harel

سلبوون

ئەڤرۆ تو دگەل منی ئەم جۆتین
هەموو تشتێ من ئەڤرۆ جۆتە
من دو دل هەنە
دو روح
دو مێژوو و دو نیشتیمان
بچی ژی
من تێك بشكێنن
سەرك و بنێك بكەن
هەر بێهنا تە ژ من دهێت
ئەز هەر رەنگێ تە ددەم
تاما تە ددەم
من بهەلاویسن ب قەد چنارەكێ ڤە
داقوتن دێ بەلگێن تە ژ من وەریێن
تو یێ د من دا
پیتكری

Falling Apart

Today you are with me; we are a couple.
All my things are coupled.
I have two hearts
two souls
two histories and two homelands.
Even if you leave me,
and they break me,
turn me upside-down,
I will still smell of you;
will carry your colour;
taste of you.
If they hang me from a plane tree
and shake me
your leaves will fall off me;
you are grafted
to me.

Co-translators: Yaser Hassan Ali and Clémence Scalbert Yücel
Translation editor: Rinat Harel

Viyan M. Tahir

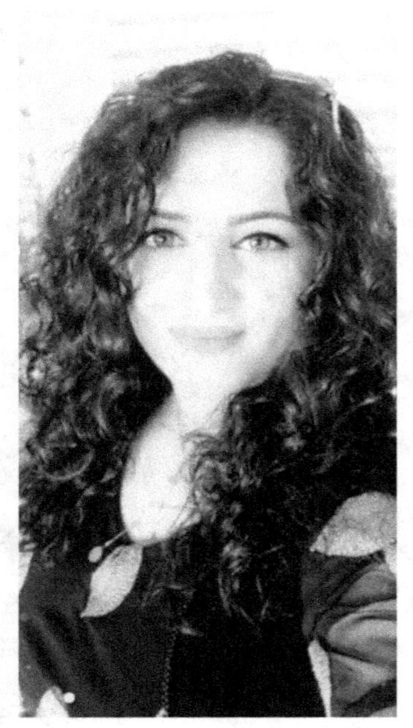

Viyan Mihemed Tahir is one of the new generation of poets who lives in Duhok, Iraqi Kurdistan. She was born in 1983 in Dêrîşkê and received her diploma in Kurdish Language in 2007. She currently works as a primary school teacher in Duhok. She began writing and publishing her poems and articles in 2012 in *Evro* daily newspaper and on social media. Her first poetry collection titled *Jinek ji Dûndeha Perperkê* (*A Woman from the Generation of Butterfly*) was published in 2020 in Duhok. Viyan is now preparing her new collection of poetry to be published in 2022.

غروور

غروورا خوه یا دەریایێ نەفرۆشە من
ئێدی ئەز ژ پێل و سیپەلا ناترسم
من چ خۆلەکێن ڤالا نینن
پێ هەناسێن کوور بهەلکێشم
دا غروورا تە پێ بکڕم
هەموو چرکێن ژیێ من ژی
یێ ب رەنگێ تە پەنگیاین
پێکۆلا من بۆ ڤالاکرنا تەیە ژ خوە
من چەند دڤێت خوە ژ تە بدزم
دا خوە د پێکێن ئەشقا من دا مەست بکەی و
ب غروورا خوە ئەژدەهایێن حەزا هار کەی
ئێدی ب دیناتیا من ب هش ناکەڤی
دێ کەنگی زانی
من ب هشێن خوە غروورا تە یا کڕی..

Ego

Do not sell me your sea-vast ego,
I no longer fear waves and waterfalls.
I have not an empty minute for
taking deep breaths
to buy your ego with.
Every second of my life
is clogged with your colour.
I try so hard to empty myself of you,
I want so much to rob you of myself,
so you get drunk on my cupful of love
and awaken the monsters of desires with your ego.
Then, you will not know my madness.
When will you see
that I bought your ego with my mind?

Translator: Yaser Hassan Ali
Translation editor: Rinat Harel

ئاوێنا خەیالێن من

ئەز و خۆلەکێن دەمی هەڤرکین
ئەز تێدا پەیڤینێن چاڤێن تە یێن مژدار
دخوینم و پێ دهەلپەرم
دا دلێ خوە پێ دیل و ژار
پێ گەنج بکەم
تو... ل سەر دەمژمێرێن بەتال دنڤی و
من کال دبینی!!
وان خەیالێن تو دگەل دپەیڤی
بایێ سحاران ل من خرڤە دکەت
گول ب خوناڤێ
ل سر رووکێ من پێ سیلاڤی دنڤێسیت و
ئاوێنا خەیالێن من ئاشکەرا دکەت و
تلێن من بەرسڤێ ددەن

The Mirror of My Dreams

The minutes are my foes.
I read in them your mysterious eyes and
dance with their words
to make my sorry heart
young again.
You…you sleep on empty hours and
think me old!!
You talk with dreams
that wrap me with the morning breeze.
The dewy flowers
write on my *Sîlavî* face,
revealing the mirror of my dreams and
my fingers answer.

[*Sîlavî* is an adjective that comes from the Kurdish word *Sîlav,* which means 'waterfall'. Note from the translator]

Translators: Yaser Hassan Ali
Translation editor: Rinat Harel

Gulîzer

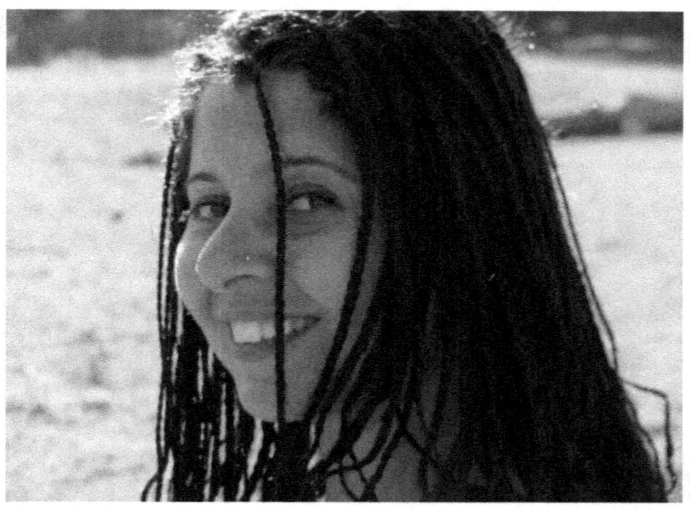

Gulîzer was born in 1979 in Amed/Diyarbakir, Northern Kurdistan. She spent several years of her childhood visiting her father, jailed for his political activities. Unable to speak Turkish as a child, she remained silent during these visits at the Diyarbakir prison, as her mother-tongue was banned. She worked as a midwife in Diyarbakir hospital for eight years. These years deepened her knowledge and experience of Kurdish women's condition and sufferings. She then became a teacher, a work she is still doing in her new country of residence, Sweden. She is the mother of two children. She is the author of four poetry collections, all published with Avesta in Istanbul: *Şevname (The Book of the Night)* in 2011, *Keziyên Jinebî (The Widow's Braids)* in 2006, *Bûka Baranê (Rainbow)* in 2009, and *Sindoqa Dirûnê (The Sewing Chest)* in 2016. All her works were published under the simple pseudonym of Gulîzer; she did not want to use a surname, which is always the one of a man, be it the father's or husband's.

Raz

Ji bo Narînê

Ez her parçeyekî xwe yê şikestî
Emanetî jineke nêzî xwe dikim
Dizanim
Her dem sindoqeke wan heye
Ji bo veşartina parçeyên şikestî û giranbuha.

The Secret

For Narîn

I entrust each of my broken parts
To a woman close to me
I know
Women always have a chest
For the safekeeping of these parts cherished and broken.

Translator: Clémence Scalbert Yücel
Translation editor: Rinat Harel

Destmal

Qederê
Bêberê
Mirov çiqas terziyekî baş be jî
Nikare destmalekê bifesilîne
Ji te.

Handkerchief

Oh, Destiny
oh, tiny offcut;
even a good tailor cannot
cut a handkerchief
from you.

Translator: Clémence Scalbert Yücel
Translation editor: Rinat Harel

Dîalekt

Her çûyîn bi hesreta mayinê
Her mayîn bi hêviya çûyinê.
Hesret û hêvî di bin konekî de
Li ser cilikekê rûdinin her tim.

Yên mayî bila nebêjin qey çûyîn hêsan e
Yên çûyî bila nebêjin qey mayîn nezan e.

Dialect

Each leaving longs for staying.
Each staying hopes for leaving.
Longing and Hope sit on a rug
under a tent—always.

May those who have stayed not say the leaving is easy.
May those who have left not say the staying is simple.

Translator: Clémence Scalbert Yücel
Translation editor: Rinat Harel

?

Ku du çem ji hev biqetin
Wê ava wan çawa ji nav hev derxin?

?

When two rivers separate
How do they part their water?

Translator: Clémence Scalbert Yücel
Translation editor: Rinat Harel

Xeyd

Ez ew zaroka ji wî qewmî,
Ez ew zaroka ku ji her qora govendê
Dor bi dor dihat qewirandin.

Ew zaroka di her dawetê de xemlandî
Golikvaniya govendê dikir
Ew zaroka bi gavên bêteşe diçû û dihat.

Ew zarok
Dilê wê her hebû ji govendê re
Lê her car
Diterikî dil jî
Govend jî.

Anger

I am that child girl from that people.
I am that child girl, turned away
from the *govend* dance, turn by turn.

That child girl, in her best dresses at wedding parties
herded the dance.
That child girl was limping around.

That child girl,
her heart was always set on the *govend*;
but each time,
the heart broke,
the *govend* broke too.

Translator: Clémence Scalbert Yücel
Translation editor: Rinat Harel

Kiras

(Di bin 40 qat kiras de veşartiye rûhê wê
Wek wan marên, di çirokên di nav sitareyan de dihatin gotin
Havînan, li ser xaniyan.)

Ne di demsalan de
Di her evîn û di her êşê de
Kirasek dirizîne û ji xwe dike.
Dor bi dor
Kirasek
Binkirasek
………………..
Kirasek
Binkirasek….

Lê hinek evîn û êş bi çil kirasan e
Hema bi derbekê ve.

Skin

(Her soul is hidden under 40 layers of skin
like the snakes in the stories, told in the quietness
of summertime, on rooftops.)

Not in the seasons;
in each love and each pain,
she peels away a skin and undresses.
One at a time.
A skin.
An underskin

……………………………..

A skin.
An underskin …….

But some loves and pains have forty skins,
all in one blow.

Translator: Clémence Scalbert Yücel
Translation editor: Rinat Harel

www.ingramcontent.com/pod-product-compliance
Lightning Source LLC
LaVergne TN
LVHW020049110826
845155LV00029B/693

* 9 7 8 1 9 1 2 9 9 7 8 1 7 *